The Poetry of Henry Wadsworth

C000008918

Volume V – In The Harbour & Other Poems

Henry Wadsworth Longfellow was born on February 27th, 1807 in Portland, Maine. As a young boy, it was obvious that he was very studious and he quickly became fluent in Latin.

He published his first poem, "The Battle of Lovell's Pond", in the Portland Gazette on November 17th, 1820. He was already thinking of a career in literature and, in his senior year, wrote to his father: "I will not disguise it in the least... the fact is, I most eagerly aspire after future eminence in literature, my whole soul burns most ardently after it, and every earthly thought centers in it...."

After graduation travels in Europe occupied the next three years and he seemed to easily absorb any language he set himself to learn.

On September 14th, 1831, Longfellow married Mary Storer Potter. They settled in Brunswick.

His first published book was in 1833, a translation of poems by the Spanish poet Jorge Manrique. He also published a travel book, Outre-Mer: A Pilgrimage Beyond the Sea.

During a trip to Europe Mary became pregnant. Sadly, in October 1835, she miscarried at some six months. After weeks of illness she died, at the age of 22 on November 29th, 1835. Longfellow wrote "One thought occupies me night and day... She is dead — She is dead! All day I am weary and sad".

In late 1839, Longfellow published Hyperion, a book in prose inspired by his trips abroad.

Ballads and Other Poems was published in 1841 and included "The Village Blacksmith" and "The Wreck of the Hesperus". His reputation as a poet, and a commercial one at that, was set.

On May 10th, 1843, after seven years in pursuit of a chance for new love, Longfellow received word from Fanny Appleton that she agreed to marry him.

On November 1st, 1847, the epic poem Evangeline was published.

In 1854, Longfellow retired from Harvard, to devote himself entirely to writing.

The Song of Haiwatha, perhaps his best known and enjoyed work was published in 1855.

On July 10th, 1861, after suffering horrific burns the previous day. In his attempts to save her Longfellow had also been badly burned and was unable to attend her funeral.

He spent several years translating Dante Alighieri's Divine Comedy. It was published in 1867.

Longfellow was also part of a group who became known as The Fireside Poets which also included William Cullen Bryant, John Greenleaf Whittier, James Russell Lowell, and Oliver Wendell Holmes Snr.

Longfellow was the most popular poet of his day. As a friend once wrote to him, "no other poet was so fully recognized in his lifetime". Some of his works including "Paul Revere's Ride" and "The Song of Haiwatha" may have rewritten the facts but became essential parts of the American psyche and culture.

Henry Wadsworth Longfellow died, surrounded by family, on Friday, March 24th, 1882. He had been suffering from peritonitis.

Index of Contents

IN THE HARBOR

BECALMED

Becalmed upon the sea of Thought,
Still unattained the land it sought,
My mind, with loosely-hanging sails,
Lies waiting the auspicious gales.

On either side, behind, before,
The ocean stretches like a floor,—
A level floor of amethyst,
Crowned by a golden dome of mist.

Blow, breath of inspiration, blow!
Shake and uplift this golden glow!
And fill the canvas of the mind
With wafts of thy celestial wind.

Blow, breath of song! until I feel
The straining sail, the lifting keel,
The life of the awakening sea,
Its motion and its mystery!

THE POET'S CALENDAR

JANUARY

Janus am I; oldest of potentates;
Forward I look, and backward, and below
I count, as god of avenues and gates,
The years that through my portals come and go.
I block the roads, and drift the fields with snow;
I chase the wild-fowl from the frozen fen;
My frosts congeal the rivers in their flow,
My fires light up the hearths and hearts of men.

FEBRUARY

I am lustration, and the sea is mine.
I wash the sands and headlands with my tide;
My brow is crowned with branches of the pine;
Before my chariot-wheels the fishes glide.
By me all things unclean are purified,
By me the souls of men washed white again;
E'en the unlovely tombs of those who died
Without a dirge, I cleanse from every stain.

MARCH

I Martius am! Once first, and now the third!
To lead the Year was my appointed place;
A mortal dispossessed me by a word,
And set there Janus with the double face.
Hence I make war on all the human race;
I shake the cities with my hurricanes;
I flood the rivers and their banks efface,
And drown the farms and hamlets with my rains.

APRIL

I open wide the portals of the Spring

To welcome the procession of the flowers,
With their gay banners, and the birds that sing
Their song of songs from their aerial towers.
I soften with my sunshine and my showers
The heart of earth; with thoughts of love I glide
Into the hearts of men; and with the Hours
Upon the Bull with wreathed horns I ride.

MAY

Hark! The sea-faring wild-fowl loud proclaim
My coming, and the swarming of the bees.
These are my heralds, and behold! my name
Is written in blossoms on the hawthorn-trees.
I tell the mariner when to sail the seas;
I waft o'er all the land from far away
The breath and bloom of the Hesperides,
My birthplace. I am Maia. I am May.

JUNE

Mine is the Month of Roses; yes, and mine
The Month of Marriages! All pleasant sights
And scents, the fragrance of the blossoming vine,
The foliage of the valleys and the heights.
Mine are the longest days, the loveliest nights;
The mower's scythe makes music to my ear;
I am the mother of all dear delights;
I am the fairest daughter of the year.

JULY

My emblem is the Lion, and I breathe
The breath of Libyan deserts o'er the land;
My sickle as a sabre I unsheathe,
And bent before me the pale harvests stand.
The lakes and rivers shrink at my command,
And there is thirst and fever in the air;
The sky is changed to brass, the earth to sand;
I am the Emperor whose name I bear.

AUGUST

The Emperor Octavian, called the August,

I being his favorite, bestowed his name
Upon me, and I hold it still in trust,
In memory of him and of his fame.
I am the Virgin, and my vestal flame
Burns less intensely than the Lion's rage;
Sheaves are my only garlands, and I claim
The golden Harvests as my heritage.

SEPTEMBER

I bear the Scales, where hang in equipoise
The night and day; and when unto my lips
I put my trumpet, with its stress and noise
Fly the white clouds like tattered sails of ships;
The tree-tops lash the air with sounding whips;
Southward the clamorous sea-fowl wing their flight;
The hedges are all red with haws and hips,
The Hunter's Moon reigns empress of the night.

OCTOBER

My ornaments are fruits; my garments leaves,
Woven like cloth of gold, and crimson dyed;
I do not boast the harvesting of sheaves,
O'er orchards and o'er vineyards I preside.
Though on the frigid Scorpion I ride,
The dreamy air is full, and overflows
With tender memories of the summer-tide,
And mingled voices of the doves and crows.

NOVEMBER

The Centaur, Sagittarius, am I,
Born of Ixion's and the cloud's embrace;
With sounding hoofs across the earth I fly,
A steed Thessalian with a human face.
Sharp winds the arrows are with which I chase
The leaves, half dead already with affright;
I shroud myself in gloom; and to the race
Of mortals bring nor comfort nor delight.

DECEMBER

Riding upon the Goat, with snow-white hair,
I come, the last of all. This crown of mine

Is of the holly; in my hand I bear
The thyrsus, tipped with fragrant cones of pine.
I celebrate the birth of the Divine,
And the return of the Saturnian reign;—
My songs are carols sung at every shrine,
Proclaiming "Peace on earth, good will to men."

AUTUMN WITHIN

It is autumn; not without,
But within me is the cold.
Youth and spring are all about;
It is I that have grown old.

Birds are darting through the air,
Singing, building without rest;
Life is stirring everywhere,
Save within my lonely breast.

There is silence: the dead leaves
Fall and rustle and are still;
Beats no flail upon the sheaves
Comes no murmur from the mill.

THE FOUR LAKES OF MADISON

Four limpid lakes,—four Naiades
Or sylvan deities are these,
In flowing robes of azure dressed;
Four lovely handmaids, that uphold
Their shining mirrors, rimmed with gold,
To the fair city in the West.

By day the coursers of the sun
Drink of these waters as they run
Their swift diurnal round on high;
By night the constellations glow
Far down the hollow deeps below,
And glimmer in another sky.

Fair lakes, serene and full of light,
Fair town, arrayed in robes of white,
How visionary ye appear!
All like a floating landscape seems

In cloud-land or the land of dreams,
Bathed in a golden atmosphere!

VICTOR AND VANQUISHED

As one who long hath fled with panting breath
Before his foe, bleeding and near to fall,
I turn and set my back against the wall,
And look thee in the face, triumphant Death,
I call for aid, and no one answereth;
I am alone with thee, who conquerest all;
Yet me thy threatening form doth not appall,
For thou art but a phantom and a wraith.
Wounded and weak, sword broken at the hilt,
With armor shattered, and without a shield,
I stand unmoved; do with me what thou wilt;
I can resist no more, but will not yield.
This is no tournament where cowards tilt;
The vanquished here is victor of the field.

MOONLIGHT

As a pale phantom with a lamp
Ascends some ruin's haunted stair,
So glides the moon along the damp
Mysterious chambers of the air.

Now hidden in cloud, and now revealed,
As if this phantom, full of pain,
Were by the crumbling walls concealed,
And at the windows seen again.

Until at last, serene and proud
In all the splendor of her light,
She walks the terraces of cloud,
Supreme as Empress of the Night.

I look, but recognize no more
Objects familiar to my view;
The very pathway to my door
Is an enchanted avenue.

All things are changed. One mass of shade,
The elm-trees drop their curtains down;

By palace, park, and colonnade
I walk as in a foreign town.

The very ground beneath my feet
Is clothed with a diviner air;
White marble paves the silent street
And glimmers in the empty square.

Illusion! Underneath there lies
The common life of every day;
Only the spirit glorifies
With its own tints the sober gray.

In vain we look, in vain uplift
Our eyes to heaven, if we are blind,
We see but what we have the gift
Of seeing; what we bring we find.

THE CHILDREN'S CRUSADE

[A FRAGMENT.]

I

What is this I read in history,
Full of marvel, full of mystery,
Difficult to understand?
Is it fiction, is it truth?
Children in the flower of youth,
Heart in heart, and hand in hand,
Ignorant of what helps or harms,
Without armor, without arms,
Journeying to the Holy Land!

Who shall answer or divine?
Never since the world was made
Such a wonderful crusade
Started forth for Palestine.
Never while the world shall last
Will it reproduce the past;
Never will it see again
Such an army, such a band,
Over mountain, over main,
Journeying to the Holy Land.

Like a shower of blossoms blown

From the parent trees were they;
Like a flock of birds that fly
Through the unfrequented sky,
Holding nothing as their own,
Passed they into lands unknown,
Passed to suffer and to die.

O the simple, child-like trust!
O the faith that could believe
What the harnessed, iron-mailed
Knights of Christendom had failed,
By their prowess, to achieve,
They the children, could and must?

Little thought the Hermit, preaching
Holy Wars to knight and baron,
That the words dropped in his teaching,
His entreaty, his beseeching,
Would by children's hands be gleaned,
And the staff on which he leaned
Blossom like the rod of Aaron.

As a summer wind upheaves
The innumerable leaves
In the bosom of a wood,—
Not as separate leaves, but massed
All together by the blast,—
So for evil or for good
His resistless breath upheaved
All at once the many-leaved,
Many-thoughted multitude.

In the tumult of the air
Rock the boughs with all the nests
Cradled on their tossing crests;
By the fervor of his prayer
Troubled hearts were everywhere
Rocked and tossed in human breasts.

For a century, at least,
His prophetic voice had ceased;
But the air was heated still
By his lurid words and will,
As from fires in far-off woods,
In the autumn of the year,
An unwonted fever broods
In the sultry atmosphere.

II

In Cologne the bells were ringing,
In Cologne the nuns were singing
Hymns and canticles divine;
Loud the monks sang in their stalls,
And the thronging streets were loud
With the voices of the crowd;—
Underneath the city walls
Silent flowed the river Rhine.

From the gates, that summer day,
Clad in robes of hodden gray,
With the red cross on the breast,
Azure-eyed and golden-haired,
Forth the young crusaders fared;
While above the band devoted
Consecrated banners floated,
Fluttered many a flag and streamer,
And the cross o'er all the rest!
Singing lowly, meekly, slowly,
"Give us, give us back the holy
Sepulchre of the Redeemer!"
On the vast procession pressed,
Youths and maidens. . . .

III

Ah! what master hand shall paint
How they journeyed on their way,
How the days grew long and dreary,
How their little feet grew weary,
How their little hearts grew faint!

Ever swifter day by day
Flowed the homeward river; ever
More and more its whitening current
Broke and scattered into spray,
Till the calmly-flowing river
Changed into a mountain torrent,
Rushing from its glacier green
Down through chasm and black ravine.
Like a phoenix in its nest,
Burned the red sun in the West,
Sinking in an ashen cloud;
In the East, above the crest

Of the sea-like mountain chain,
Like a phoenix from its shroud,
Came the red sun back again.

Now around them, white with snow,
Closed the mountain peaks. Below,
Headlong from the precipice
Down into the dark abyss,
Plunged the cataract, white with foam;
And it said, or seemed to say:
"Oh return, while yet you may,
Foolish children, to your home,
There the Holy City is!"

But the dauntless leader said:
"Faint not, though your bleeding feet
O'er these slippery paths of sleet
Move but painfully and slowly;
Other feet than yours have bled;
Other tears than yours been shed
Courage! lose not heart or hope;
On the mountains' southern slope
Lies Jerusalem the Holy!"

As a white rose in its pride,
By the wind in summer-tide
Tossed and loosened from the branch,
Showers its petals o'er the ground,
From the distant mountain's side,
Scattering all its snows around,
With mysterious, muffled sound,
Loosened, fell the avalanche.
Voices, echoes far and near,
Roar of winds and waters blending,
Mists uprising, clouds impending,
Filled them with a sense of fear,
Formless, nameless, never ending.

SUNDOWN

The summer sun is sinking low;
Only the tree-tops redden and glow:
Only the weathercock on the spire
Of the neighboring church is a flame of fire;
All is in shadow below.

O beautiful, awful summer day,
What hast thou given, what taken away?
Life and death, and love and hate,
Homes made happy or desolate,
Hearts made sad or gay!

On the road of life one mile-stone more!
In the book of life one leaf turned o'er!
Like a red seal is the setting sun
On the good and the evil men have done,—
Naught can to-day restore!

CHIMES

Sweet chimes! that in the loneliness of night
Salute the passing hour, and in the dark
And silent chambers of the household mark
The movements of the myriad orbs of light!
Through my closed eyelids, by the inner sight,
I see the constellations in the arc
Of their great circles moving on, and hark!
I almost hear them singing in their flight.
Better than sleep it is to lie awake
O'er-canopied by the vast starry dome
Of the immeasurable sky; to feel
The slumbering world sink under us, and make
Hardly an eddy,—a mere rush of foam
On the great sea beneath a sinking keel.

FOUR BY THE CLOCK

"Nahant, September 8, 1880,
Four o'clock in the morning."

Four by the clock! and yet not day;
But the great world rolls and wheels away,
With its cities on land, and its ships at sea,
Into the dawn that is to be!

Only the lamp in the anchored bark
Sends its glimmer across the dark,
And the heavy breathing of the sea
Is the only sound that comes to me.

AUF WIEDERSEHEN

IN MEMORY OF J.T.F.

Until we meet again! That is the meaning
Of the familiar words, that men repeat
At parting in the street.
Ah yes, till then! but when death intervening
Rends us asunder, with what ceaseless pain
We wait for the Again!

The friends who leave us do not feel the sorrow
Of parting, as we feel it, who must stay
Lamenting day by day,
And knowing, when we wake upon the morrow,
We shall not find in its accustomed place
The one beloved face.

It were a double grief, if the departed,
Being released from earth, should still retain
A sense of earthly pain;
It were a double grief, if the true-hearted,
Who loved us here, should on the farther shore
Remember us no more.

Believing, in the midst of our afflictions,
That death is a beginning, not an end,
We cry to them, and send
Farewells, that better might be called predictions,
Being fore-shadowings of the future, thrown
Into the vast Unknown.

Faith overleaps the confines of our reason,
And if by faith, as in old times was said,
Women received their dead
Raised up to life, then only for a season
Our partings are, nor shall we wait in vain
Until we meet again!

ELEGIAC VERSE

I

Peradventure of old, some bard in Ionian Islands,

Walking alone by the sea, hearing the wash of the waves,
Learned the secret from them of the beautiful verse elegiac,
Breathing into his song motion and sound of the sea.

For as the wave of the sea, upheaving in long undulations,
Plunges loud on the sands, pauses, and turns, and retreats,
So the Hexameter, rising and singing, with cadence sonorous,
Falls; and in refluent rhythm back the Pentameter flows?

II

Not in his youth alone, but in age, may the heart of the poet
Bloom into song, as the gorse blossoms in autumn and spring.

III

Not in tenderness wanting, yet rough are the rhymes of our poet;
Though it be Jacob's voice, Esau's, alas! are the hands.

IV

Let us be grateful to writers for what is left in the inkstand;
When to leave off is an art only attained by the few.

V

How can the Three be One? you ask me; I answer by asking,
Hail and snow and rain, are they not three, and yet one?

VI

By the mirage uplifted the land floats vague in the ether,
Ships and the shadows of ships hang in the motionless air;
So by the art of the poet our common life is uplifted,
So, transfigured, the world floats in a luminous haze.

VII

Like a French poem is Life; being only perfect in structure
When with the masculine rhymes mingled the feminine are.

VIII

Down from the mountain descends the brooklet, rejoicing in freedom;
Little it dreams of the mill hid in the valley below;
Glad with the joy of existence, the child goes singing and laughing,
Little dreaming what toils lie in the future concealed.

IX

As the ink from our pen, so flow our thoughts and our feelings
When we begin to write, however sluggish before.

X

Like the Kingdom of Heaven, the Fountain of Youth is within us;
If we seek it elsewhere, old shall we grow in the search.

XI

If you would hit the mark, you must aim a little above it;
Every arrow that flies feels the attraction of earth.

XII

Wisely the Hebrews admit no Present tense in their language;
While we are speaking the word, it is is already the Past.

XIII

In the twilight of age all things seem strange and phantasmal,
As between daylight and dark ghost-like the landscape appears.

XIV

Great is the art of beginning, but greater the art is of ending;
Many a poem is marred by a superfluous verse.

THE CITY AND THE SEA

The panting City cried to the Sea,
"I am faint with heat,—O breathe on me!"

And the Sea said, "Lo, I breathe! but my breath
To some will be life, to others death!"

As to Prometheus, bringing ease
In pain, come the Oceanides,

So to the City, hot with the flame
Of the pitiless sun, the east wind came.

It came from the heaving breast of the deep,
Silent as dreams are, and sudden as sleep.

Life-giving, death-giving, which will it be;
O breath of the merciful, merciless Sea?

MEMORIES

Oft I remember those whom I have known
In other days, to whom my heart was led
As by a magnet, and who are not dead,
But absent, and their memories overgrown
With other thoughts and troubles of my own,
As graves with grasses are, and at their head
The stone with moss and lichens so o'erspread,
Nothing is legible but the name alone.
And is it so with them? After long years,
Do they remember me in the same way,
And is the memory pleasant as to me?
I fear to ask; yet wherefore are my fears?
Pleasures, like flowers, may wither and decay,
And yet the root perennial may be.

HERMES TRISMEGISTUS

*As Seleucus narrates, Hermes describes the principles that rank as wholes in two myriads of books; or, as we are informed by Manetho, he perfectly unfolded these principles in three myriads six thousand five hundred and twenty-five volumes. . . . . . . Our ancestors dedicated the inventions of their wisdom to this deity, inscribing all their own writings with the name of Hermes.—**IAMBLICUS**.*

Still through Egypt's desert places
Flows the lordly Nile,
From its banks the great stone faces
Gaze with patient smile.
Still the pyramids imperious
Pierce the cloudless skies,
And the Sphinx stares with mysterious,
Solemn, stony eyes.

But where are the old Egyptian
Demi-gods and kings?
Nothing left but an inscription
Graven on stones and rings.
Where are Helios and Hephaestus,
Gods of eldest eld?
Where is Hermes Trismegistus,

Who their secrets held?

Where are now the many hundred
Thousand books he wrote?
By the Thaumaturgists plundered,
Lost in lands remote;
In oblivion sunk forever,
As when o'er the land
Blows a storm-wind, in the river
Sinks the scattered sand.

Something unsubstantial, ghostly,
Seems this Theurgist,
In deep meditation mostly
Wrapped, as in a mist.
Vague, phantasmal, and unreal
To our thought he seems,
Walking in a world ideal,
In a land of dreams.

Was he one, or many, merging
Name and fame in one,
Like a stream, to which, converging
Many streamlets run?
Till, with gathered power proceeding,
Ampler sweep it takes,
Downward the sweet waters leading
From unnumbered lakes.

By the Nile I see him wandering,
Pausing now and then,
On the mystic union pondering
Between gods and men;
Half believing, wholly feeling,
With supreme delight,
How the gods, themselves concealing,
Lift men to their height.

Or in Thebes, the hundred-gated,
In the thoroughfare
Breathing, as if consecrated,
A diviner air;
And amid discordant noises,
In the jostling throng,
Hearing far, celestial voices
Of Olympian song.

Who shall call his dreams fallacious?

Who has searched or sought
All the unexplored and spacious
Universe of thought?
Who, in his own skill confiding,
Shall with rule and line
Mark the border-land dividing
Human and divine?

Trismegistus! three times greatest!
How thy name sublime
Has descended to this latest
Progeny of time!
Happy they whose written pages
Perish with their lives,
If amid the crumbling ages
Still their name survives!

Thine, O priest of Egypt, lately
Found I in the vast,
Weed-encumbered sombre, stately,
Grave-yard of the Past;
And a presence moved before me
On that gloomy shore,
As a waft of wind, that o'er me
Breathed, and was no more.

TO THE AVON

Flow on, sweet river! like his verse
Who lies beneath this sculptured hearse
Nor wait beside the churchyard wall
For him who cannot hear thy call.

Thy playmate once; I see him now
A boy with sunshine on his brow,
And hear in Stratford's quiet street
The patter of his little feet.

I see him by thy shallow edge
Wading knee-deep amid the sedge;
And lost in thought, as if thy stream
Were the swift river of a dream.

He wonders whitherward it flows;
And fain would follow where it goes,
To the wide world, that shall erelong

Be filled with his melodious song.

Flow on, fair stream! That dream is o'er;
He stands upon another shore;
A vaster river near him flows,
And still he follows where it goes.

PRESIDENT GARFIELD

"E venni dal martirio a questa pace."

These words the poet heard in Paradise,
Uttered by one who, bravely dying here,
In the true faith was living in that sphere
Where the celestial cross of sacrifice
Spread its protecting arms athwart the skies;
And set thereon, like jewels crystal clear,
The souls magnanimous, that knew not fear,
Flashed their effulgence on his dazzled eyes.
Ah me! how dark the discipline of pain,
Were not the suffering followed by the sense
Of infinite rest and infinite release!
This is our consolation; and again
A great soul cries to us in our suspense,
"I came from martyrdom unto this peace!"

MY BOOKS

Sadly as some old mediaeval knight
Gazed at the arms he could no longer wield,
The sword two-handed and the shining shield
Suspended in the hall, and full in sight,
While secret longings for the lost delight
Of tourney or adventure in the field
Came over him, and tears but half concealed
Trembled and fell upon his beard of white,
So I behold these books upon their shelf,
My ornaments and arms of other days;
Not wholly useless, though no longer used,
For they remind me of my other self,
Younger and stronger, and the pleasant ways
In which I walked, now clouded and confused.

IN THE WHITE MOUNTAINS

TRAVELLER

Why dost thou wildly rush and roar,
Mad River, O Mad River?
Wilt thou not pause and cease to pour
Thy hurrying, headlong waters o'er
This rocky shelf forever?

What secret trouble stirs thy breast?
Why all this fret and flurry?
Dost thou not know that what is best
In this too restless world is rest
From over-work and worry?

THE RIVER

What wouldst thou in these mountains seek,
O stranger from the city?
Is it perhaps some foolish freak
Of thine, to put the words I speak
Into a plaintive ditty?

TRAVELLER

Yes; I would learn of thee thy song,
With all its flowing number;
And in a voice as fresh and strong
As thine is, sing it all day long,
And hear it in my slumbers.

THE RIVER

A brooklet nameless and unknown
Was I at first, resembling
A little child, that all alone
Comes venturing down the stairs of stone,
Irresolute and trembling.

Later, by wayward fancies led,
For the wide world I panted;
Out of the forest dark and dread
Across the open fields I fled,
Like one pursued and haunted.

I tossed my arms, I sang aloud,
My voice exultant blending
With thunder from the passing cloud,

The wind, the forest bent and bowed,
The rush of rain descending.

I heard the distant ocean call,
Imploring and entreating;
Drawn onward, o'er this rocky wall
I plunged, and the loud waterfall
Made answer to the greeting.

And now, beset with many ills,
A toilsome life I follow;
Compelled to carry from the hills
These logs to the impatient mills
Below there in the hollow.

Yet something ever cheers and charms
The rudeness of my labors;
Daily I water with these arms
The cattle of a hundred farms,
And have the birds for neighbors.

Men call me Mad, and well they may,
When, full of rage and trouble,
I burst my banks of sand and clay,
And sweep their wooden bridge away,
Like withered reeds or stubble.

Now go and write thy little rhyme,
As of thine own creating.
Thou seest the day is past its prime;
I can no longer waste my time;
The mills are tired of waiting.

POSSIBILITIES

Where are the Poets, unto whom belong
The Olympian heights; whose singing shafts were sent
Straight to the mark, and not from bows half bent,
But with the utmost tension of the thong?
Where are the stately argosies of song,
Whose rushing keels made music as they went
Sailing in search of some new continent,
With all sail set, and steady winds and strong?
Perhaps there lives some dreamy boy, untaught
In schools, some graduate of the field or street,
Who shall become a master of the art,

An admiral sailing the high seas of thought,
Fearless and first and steering with his fleet
For lands not yet laid down in any chart.

DECORATION DAY

Sleep, comrades, sleep and rest
On this Field of the Grounded Arms,
Where foes no more molest,
Nor sentry's shot alarms!

Ye have slept on the ground before,
And started to your feet
At the cannon's sudden roar,
Or the drum's redoubling beat.

But in this camp of Death
No sound your slumber breaks;
Here is no fevered breath,
No wound that bleeds and aches.

All is repose and peace,
Untrampled lies the sod;
The shouts of battle cease,
It is the Truce of God!

Rest, comrades, rest and sleep!
The thoughts of men shall be
As sentinels to keep
Your rest from danger free.

Your silent tents of green
We deck with fragrant flowers;
Yours has the suffering been,
The memory shall be ours.

A FRAGMENT

Awake! arise! the hour is late!
Angels are knocking at thy door!
They are in haste and cannot wait,
And once departed come no more.

Awake! arise! the athlete's arm

Loses its strength by too much rest;
The fallow land, the untilled farm
Produces only weeds at best.

LOSS AND GAIN

When I compare
What I have lost with what I have gained,
What I have missed with what attained,
Little room do I find for pride.

I am aware
How many days have been idly spent;
How like an arrow the good intent
Has fallen short or been turned aside.

But who shall dare
To measure loss and gain in this wise?
Defeat may be victory in disguise;
The lowest ebb is the turn of the tide.

INSCRIPTION ON THE SHANKLIN FOUNTAIN

O traveller, stay thy weary feet;
Drink of this fountain, pure and sweet;
It flows for rich and poor the same.
Then go thy way, remembering still
The wayside well beneath the hill,
The cup of water in His name.

THE BELLS OF SAN BLAS

What say the Bells of San Blas
To the ships that southward pass
From the harbor of Mazatlan?
To them it is nothing more
Than the sound of surf on the shore, —
Nothing more to master or man.

But to me, a dreamer of dreams,
To whom what is and what seems
Are often one and the same, —

The Bells of San Blas to me
Have a strange, wild melody,
And are something more than a name.

For bells are the voice of the church;
They have tones that touch and search
The hearts of young and old;
One sound to all, yet each
Lends a meaning to their speech,
And the meaning is manifold.

They are a voice of the Past,
Of an age that is fading fast,
Of a power austere and grand,
When the flag of Spain unfurled
Its folds o'er this western world,
And the Priest was lord of the land.

The chapel that once looked down
On the little seaport town
Has crumbled into the dust;
And on oaken beams below
The bells swing to and fro,
And are green with mould and rust.

"Is, then, the old faith dead,"
They say, "and in its stead
Is some new faith proclaimed,
That we are forced to remain
Naked to sun and rain,
Unsheltered and ashamed?

"Once, in our tower aloof,
We rang over wall and roof
Our warnings and our complaints;
And round about us there
The white doves filled the air,
Like the white souls of the saints.

"The saints! Ah, have they grown
Forgetful of their own?
Are they asleep, or dead,
That open to the sky
Their ruined Missions lie,
No longer tenanted?

"Oh, bring us back once more
The vanished days of yore,

When the world with faith was filled;
Bring back the fervid zeal,
The hearts of fire and steel,
The hands that believe and build.

"Then from our tower again
We will send over land and main
Our voices of command,
Like exiled kings who return
To their thrones, and the people learn
That the Priest is lord of the land!"

O Bells of San Blas in vain
Ye call back the Past again;
The Past is deaf to your prayer!
Out of the shadows of night
The world rolls into light;
It is daybreak everywhere.

TRANSLATIONS

Longfellow was an excellent translator and could work across many languages. Perhaps his best work was Dante's The Divine Comedy but the samples below illustrate the breadth of his talent.

PRELUDE

As treasures that men seek,
Deep-buried in sea-sands,
Vanish if they but speak,
And elude their eager hands,

So ye escape and slip,
O songs, and fade away,
When the word is on my lip
To interpret what ye say.

Were it not better, then,
To let the treasures rest
Hid from the eyes of men,
Locked in their iron chest?

I have but marked the place,
But half the secret told,
That, following this slight trace,
Others may find the gold.

THE CELESTIAL PILOT

PURGATORIO II. 13-51.

And now, behold! as at the approach of morning,
Through the gross vapors, Mars grows fiery red
Down in the west upon the ocean floor
Appeared to me,—may I again behold it!
A light along the sea, so swiftly coming,
Its motion by no flight of wing is equalled.
And when therefrom I had withdrawn a little
Mine eyes, that I might question my conductor,
Again I saw it brighter grown and larger.
Thereafter, on all sides of it, appeared
I knew not what of white, and underneath,
Little by little, there came forth another.
My master yet had uttered not a word,
While the first whiteness into wings unfolded;
But, when he clearly recognized the pilot,
He cried aloud: "Quick, quick, and bow the knee!
Behold the Angel of God! fold up thy hands!
Henceforward shalt thou see such officers!
See, how he scorns all human arguments,
So that no oar he wants, nor other sail
Than his own wings, between so distant shores!
See, how he holds them, pointed straight to heaven,
Fanning the air with the eternal pinions,
That do not moult themselves like mortal hair!"
And then, as nearer and more near us came
The Bird of Heaven, more glorious he appeared,
So that the eye could not sustain his presence,
But down I cast it; and he came to shore
With a small vessel, gliding swift and light,
So that the water swallowed naught thereof.
Upon the stern stood the Celestial Pilot!
Beatitude seemed written in his face!
And more than a hundred spirits sat within.
"In exitu Israel de Aegypto!"
Thus sang they all together in one voice,
With whatso in that Psalm is after written.

Then made he sign of holy rood upon them,
Whereat all cast themselves upon the shore,
And he departed swiftly as he came.

THE TERRESTRIAL PARADISE

PURGATORIO XXVIII. 1-33.

Longing already to search in and round
The heavenly forest, dense and living-green,
Which tempered to the eyes the newborn day,
Withouten more delay I left the bank,
Crossing the level country slowly, slowly,
Over the soil, that everywhere breathed fragrance.
A gently-breathing air, that no mutation
Had in itself, smote me upon the forehead,
No heavier blow, than of a pleasant breeze,
Whereat the tremulous branches readily
Did all of them bow downward towards that side
Where its first shadow casts the Holy Mountain;
Yet not from their upright direction bent
So that the little birds upon their tops
Should cease the practice of their tuneful art;
But with full-throated joy, the hours of prime
Singing received they in the midst of foliage
That made monotonous burden to their rhymes,
Even as from branch to branch it gathering swells,
Through the pine forests on the shore of Chiassi,
When Aeolus unlooses the Sirocco.
Already my slow steps had led me on
Into the ancient wood so far, that I
Could see no more the place where I had entered.
And lo! my further course cut off a river,
Which, tow'rds the left hand, with its little waves,
Bent down the grass, that on its margin sprang.
All waters that on earth most limpid are,
Would seem to have within themselves some mixture,
Compared with that, which nothing doth conceal,
Although it moves on with a brown, brown current,
Under the shade perpetual, that never
Ray of the sun lets in, nor of the moon.

BEATRICE

PURGATORIO XXX. 13-33, 85-99, XXXI. 13-21.

Even as the Blessed, at the final summons,
Shall rise up quickened, each one from his grave,
Wearing again the garments of the flesh,
So, upon that celestial chariot,
A hundred rose ad vocem tanti senis,
Ministers and messengers of life eternal.
They all were saying, "Benedictus qui venis,"
And scattering flowers above and round about,
"Manibus o date lilia plenis."
Oft have I seen, at the approach of day,
The orient sky all stained with roseate hues,
And the other heaven with light serene adorned,
And the sun's face uprising, overshadowed,
So that, by temperate influence of vapors,
The eye sustained his aspect for long while;
Thus in the bosom of a cloud of flowers,
Which from those hands angelic were thrown up,
And down descended inside and without,
With crown of olive o'er a snow-white veil,
Appeared a lady, under a green mantle,
Vested in colors of the living flame.

Even as the snow, among the living rafters
Upon the back of Italy, congeals,
Blown on and beaten by Sclavonian winds,
And then, dissolving, filters through itself,
Whene'er the land, that loses shadow, breathes,
Like as a taper melts before a fire,
Even such I was, without a sigh or tear,
Before the song of those who chime forever
After the chiming of the eternal spheres;
But, when I heard in those sweet melodies
Compassion for me, more than had they said,
"O wherefore, lady, dost thou thus consume him?"
The ice, that was about my heart congealed,
To air and water changed, and, in my anguish,
Through lips and eyes came gushing from my breast.

Confusion and dismay, together mingled,
Forced such a feeble "Yes!" out of my mouth,
To understand it one had need of sight.
Even as a cross-bow breaks, when 't is discharged,
Too tensely drawn the bow-string and the bow,
And with less force the arrow hits the mark;
So I gave way beneath this heavy burden,
Gushing forth into bitter tears and sighs,

And the voice, fainting, flagged upon its passage.

TO ITALY

BY VINCENZO DA FILICAJA

Italy! Italy! thou who'rt doomed to wear
The fatal gift of beauty, and possess
The dower funest of infinite wretchedness
Written upon thy forehead by despair;
Ah! would that thou wert stronger, or less fair.
That they might fear thee more, or love thee less,
Who in the splendor of thy loveliness
Seem wasting, yet to mortal combat dare!
Then from the Alps I should not see descending
Such torrents of armed men, nor Gallic horde
Drinking the wave of Po, distained with gore,
Nor should I see thee girded with a sword
Not thine, and with the stranger's arm contending,
Victor or vanquished, slave forever more.

SEVEN SONNETS AND A CANZONE

The following translations are from the poems of Michael Angelo as revised by his nephew Michael Angelo the Younger, and were made before the publication of the original text by Guasti.

I

THE ARTIST

Nothing the greatest artist can conceive
That every marble block doth not confine
Within itself; and only its design
The hand that follows intellect can achieve.
The ill I flee, the good that I believe,
In thee, fair lady, lofty and divine,
Thus hidden lie; and so that death be mine
Art, of desired success, doth me bereave.
Love is not guilty, then, nor thy fair face,
Nor fortune, cruelty, nor great disdain,
Of my disgrace, nor chance, nor destiny,
If in thy heart both death and love find place
At the same time, and if my humble brain,
Burning, can nothing draw but death from thee.

II

FIRE

Not without fire can any workman mould
The iron to his preconceived design,
Nor can the artist without fire refine
And purify from all its dross the gold;
Nor can revive the phoenix, we are told,
Except by fire. Hence if such death be mine
I hope to rise again with the divine,
Whom death augments, and time cannot make old.
O sweet, sweet death! O fortunate fire that burns
Within me still to renovate my days,
Though I am almost numbered with the dead!
If by its nature unto heaven returns
This element, me, kindled in its blaze,
Will it bear upward when my life is fled.

III

YOUTH AND AGE

Oh give me back the days when loose and free
To my blind passion were the curb and rein,
Oh give me back the angelic face again,
With which all virtue buried seems to be!
Oh give my panting footsteps back to me,
That are in age so slow and fraught with pain,
And fire and moisture in the heart and brain,
If thou wouldst have me burn and weep for thee!
If it be true thou livest alone, Amor,
On the sweet-bitter tears of human hearts,
In an old man thou canst not wake desire;
Souls that have almost reached the other shore
Of a diviner love should feel the darts,
And be as tinder to a holier fire.

IV

OLD AGE

The course of my long life hath reached at last,
In fragile bark o'er a tempestuous sea,
The common harbor, where must rendered be
Account of all the actions of the past.
The impassioned phantasy, that, vague and vast,
Made art an idol and a king to me,
Was an illusion, and but vanity
Were the desires that lured me and harassed.
The dreams of love, that were so sweet of yore,
What are they now, when two deaths may be mine,—
One sure, and one forecasting its alarms?
Painting and sculpture satisfy no more
The soul now turning to the Love Divine,
That oped, to embrace us, on the cross its arms.

V

TO VITTORIA COLONNA

Lady, how can it chance—yet this we see
In long experience—that will longer last
A living image carved from quarries vast
Than its own maker, who dies presently?
Cause yieldeth to effect if this so be,
And even Nature is by Art at surpassed;
This know I, who to Art have given the past,
But see that Time is breaking faith with me.
Perhaps on both of us long life can I
Either in color or in stone bestow,
By now portraying each in look and mien;
So that a thousand years after we die,
How fair thou wast, and I how full of woe,
And wherefore I so loved thee, may be seen.

VI

TO VITTORIA COLONNA

When the prime mover of my many sighs
Heaven took through death from out her earthly place,
Nature, that never made so fair a face,
Remained ashamed, and tears were in all eyes.
O fate, unheeding my impassioned cries!

O hopes fallacious! O thou spirit of grace,
Where art thou now? Earth holds in its embrace
Thy lovely limbs, thy holy thoughts the skies.
Vainly did cruel death attempt to stay
The rumor of thy virtuous renown,
That Lethe's waters could not wash away!
A thousand leaves, since he hath stricken thee down,
Speak of thee, nor to thee could Heaven convey,
Except through death, a refuge and a crown.

VII

DANTE

What should be said of him cannot be said;
By too great splendor is his name attended;
To blame is easier those who him offended,
Than reach the faintest glory round him shed.
This man descended to the doomed and dead
For our instruction; then to God ascended;
Heaven opened wide to him its portals splendid,
Who from his country's, closed against him, fled.
Ungrateful land! To its own prejudice
Nurse of his fortunes; and this showeth well,
That the most perfect most of grief shall see.
Among a thousand proofs let one suffice,
That as his exile hath no parallel,
Ne'er walked the earth a greater man than he.

VIII

CANZONE

Ah me! ah me! when thinking of the years,
The vanished years, alas, I do not find
Among them all one day that was my own!
Fallacious hope; desires of the unknown,
Lamenting, loving, burning, and in tears
(For human passions all have stirred my mind),
Have held me, now I feel and know, confined
Both from the true and good still far away.
I perish day by day;
The sunshine fails, the shadows grow more dreary,
And I am near to fail, infirm and weary.

THE NATURE OF LOVE

BY GUIDO GUINIZELLI

To noble heart Love doth for shelter fly,
As seeks the bird the forest's leafy shade;
Love was not felt till noble heart beat high,
Nor before love the noble heart was made.
Soon as the sun's broad flame
Was formed, so soon the clear light filled the air;
Yet was not till he came:
So love springs up in noble breasts, and there
Has its appointed space,
As heat in the bright flames finds its allotted place.
Kindles in noble heart the fire of love,
As hidden virtue in the precious stone:
This virtue comes not from the stars above,
Till round it the ennobling sun has shone;
But when his powerful blaze
Has drawn forth what was vile, the stars impart
Strange virtue in their rays;
And thus when Nature doth create the heart
Noble and pure and high,
Like virtue from the star, love comes from woman's eye.

FROM THE PORTUGUESE

SONG

BY GIL VICENTE

If thou art sleeping, maiden,
Awake and open thy door,
'T is the break of day, and we must away,
O'er meadow, and mount, and moor.

Wait not to find thy slippers,
But come with thy naked feet;
We shall have to pass through the dewy grass,
And waters wide and fleet.

VIRGIL'S FIRST ECLOGUE

MELIBOEUS
Tityrus, thou in the shade of a spreading beech-tree reclining,
Meditatest, with slender pipe, the Muse of the woodlands.
We our country's bounds and pleasant pastures relinquish,
We our country fly; thou, Tityrus, stretched in the shadow,
Teachest the woods to resound with the name of the fair Amaryllis.

TITYRUS
O Meliboeus, a god for us this leisure created,
For he will be unto me a god forever; his altar
Oftentimes shall imbue a tender lamb from our sheepfolds.
He, my heifers to wander at large, and myself, as thou seest,
On my rustic reed to play what I will, hath permitted.

MELIBOEUS
Truly I envy not, I marvel rather; on all sides
In all the fields is such trouble. Behold, my goats I am driving,
Heartsick, further away; this one scarce, Tityrus, lead I;
For having here yeaned twins just now among the dense hazels,
Hope of the flock, ah me! on the naked flint she hath left them.
Often this evil to me, if my mind had not been insensate,
Oak-trees stricken by heaven predicted, as now I remember;
Often the sinister crow from the hollow ilex predicted,
Nevertheless, who this god may be, O Tityrus, tell me.

TITYRUS
O Meliboeus, the city that they call Rome, I imagined,
Foolish I! to be like this of ours, where often we shepherds
Wonted are to drive down of our ewes the delicate offspring.
Thus whelps like unto dogs had I known, and kids to their mothers,
Thus to compare great things with small had I been accustomed.
But this among other cities its head as far hath exalted
As the cypresses do among the lissome viburnums.

MELIBOEUS
And what so great occasion of seeing Rome hath possessed thee?

TITYRUS
Liberty, which, though late, looked upon me in my inertness,
After the time when my beard fell whiter front me in shaving,—
Yet she looked upon me, and came to me after a long while,
Since Amaryllis possesses and Galatea hath left me.
For I will even confess that while Galatea possessed me
Neither care of my flock nor hope of liberty was there.

Though from my wattled folds there went forth many a victim,
And the unctuous cheese was pressed for the city ungrateful,
Never did my right hand return home heavy with money.

MELIBOEUS

I have wondered why sad thou invokedst the gods, Amaryllis,
And for whom thou didst suffer the apples to hang on the branches!
Tityrus hence was absent! Thee, Tityrus, even the pine-trees,
Thee, the very fountains, the very copses were calling.

TITYRUS

What could I do? No power had I to escape from my bondage,
Nor had I power elsewhere to recognize gods so propitious.
Here I beheld that youth, to whom each year, Meliboeus,
During twice six days ascends the smoke of our altars.
Here first gave he response to me soliciting favor:
"Feed as before your heifers, ye boys, and yoke up your bullocks."

MELIBOEUS

Fortunate old man! So then thy fields will be left thee,
And large enough for thee, though naked stone and the marish
All thy pasture-lands with the dreggy rush may encompass.
No unaccustomed food thy gravid ewes shall endanger,
Nor of the neighboring flock the dire contagion inject them.
Fortunate old man! Here among familiar rivers,
And these sacred founts, shalt thou take the shadowy coolness.
On this side, a hedge along the neighboring cross-road,
Where Hyblaean bees ever feed on the flower of the willow,
Often with gentle susurrus to fall asleep shall persuade thee.
Yonder, beneath the high rock, the pruner shall sing to the breezes,
Nor meanwhile shalt thy heart's delight, the hoarse wood-pigeons,
Nor the turtle-dove cease to mourn from aerial elm-trees.

TITYRUS

Therefore the agile stags shall sooner feed in the ether,
And the billows leave the fishes bare on the sea-shore.
Sooner, the border-lands of both overpassed, shall the exiled
Parthian drink of the Soane, or the German drink of the Tigris,
Than the face of him shall glide away from my bosom!

MELIBOEUS

But we hence shall go, a part to the thirsty Afries,
Part to Scythia come, and the rapid Cretan Oaxes,
And to the Britons from all the universe utterly sundered.
Ah, shall I ever, a long time hence, the bounds of my country
And the roof of my lowly cottage covered with greensward
Seeing, with wonder behold,—my kingdoms, a handful of wheat-ears!
Shall an impious soldier possess these lands newly cultured,

And these fields of corn a barbarian? Lo, whither discord
Us wretched people hath brought! for whom our fields we have planted!
Graft, Meliboeus, thy pear-trees now, put in order thy vine-yards.
Go, my goats, go hence, my flocks so happy aforetime.
Never again henceforth outstretched in my verdurous cavern
Shall I behold you afar from the bushy precipice hanging.
Songs no more shall I sing; not with me, ye goats, as your shepherd,
Shall ye browse on the bitter willow or blooming laburnum.

TITYRUS

Nevertheless, this night together with me canst thou rest thee
Here on the verdant leaves; for us there are mellowing apples,
Chestnuts soft to the touch, and clouted cream in abundance;
And the high roofs now of the villages smoke in the distance,
And from the lofty mountains are falling larger the shadows.

OVID IN EXILE

AT TOMIS, IN BESSARABIA, NEAR THE MOUTHS OF THE DANUBE

TRISTIA, Book III, Elegy X.

Should any one there in Rome remember Ovid the exile,
And, without me, my name still in the city survive;

Tell him that under stars which never set in the ocean
I am existing still, here in a barbarous land.

Fierce Sarmatians encompass me round, and the Bessi and Getae;
Names how unworthy to be sung by a genius like mine!

Yet when the air is warm, intervening Ister defends us:
He, as he flows, repels inroads of war with his waves.

But when the dismal winter reveals its hideous aspect,
When all the earth becomes white with a marble-like frost;

And when Boreas is loosed, and the snow hurled under Arcturus,
Then these nations, in sooth, shudder and shiver with cold.

Deep lies the snow, and neither the sun nor the rain can dissolve it;
Boreas hardens it still, makes it forever remain.

Hence, ere the first ha-s melted away, another succeeds it,
And two years it is wont, in many places, to lie.

And so great is the power of the Northwind awakened, it levels
Lofty towers with the ground, roofs uplifted bears off.

Wrapped in skins, and with trousers sewed, they contend with the weather,
And their faces alone of the whole body are seen.

Often their tresses, when shaken, with pendent icicles tinkle,
And their whitened beards shine with the gathering frost.

Wines consolidate stand, preserving the form of the vessels;
No more draughts of wine,—pieces presented they drink.

Why should I tell you how all the rivers are frozen and solid,
And from out of the lake frangible water is dug?

Ister,—no narrower stream than the river that bears the papyrus,—
Which through its many mouths mingles its waves with the deep;

Ister, with hardening winds, congeals its cerulean waters,
Under a roof of ice, winding its way to the sea.

There where ships have sailed, men go on foot; and the billows,
Solid made by the frost, hoof-beats of horses indent.

Over unwonted bridges, with water gliding beneath them,
The Sarmatian steers drag their barbarian carts.

Scarcely shall I be believed; yet when naught is gained by a falsehood,
Absolute credence then should to a witness be given.

I have beheld the vast Black Sea of ice all compacted,
And a slippery crust pressing its motionless tides.

'T is not enough to have seen, I have trodden this indurate ocean;
Dry shod passed my foot over its uppermost wave.

If thou hadst had of old such a sea as this is, Leander!
Then thy death had not been charged as a crime to the Strait.

Nor can the curved dolphins uplift themselves from the water;
All their struggles to rise merciless winter prevents;

And though Boreas sound with roar of wings in commotion,
In the blockaded gulf never a wave will there be;

And the ships will stand hemmed in by the frost, as in marble,
Nor will the oar have power through the stiff waters to cleave.

Fast-bound in the ice have I seen the fishes adhering,
Yet notwithstanding this some of them still were alive.

Hence, if the savage strength of omnipotent Boreas freezes
Whether the salt-sea wave, whether the refluent stream,—

Straightway,—the Ister made level by arid blasts of the North-wind,—
Comes the barbaric foe borne on his swift-footed steed;

Foe, that powerful made by his steed and his far-flying arrows,
All the neighboring land void of inhabitants makes.

Some take flight, and none being left to defend their possessions,
Unprotected, their goods pillage and plunder become;

Cattle and creaking carts, the little wealth of the country,
And what riches beside indigent peasants possess.

Some as captives are driven along, their hands bound behind them,
Looking backward in vain toward their Lares and lands.

Others, transfixed with barbed arrows, in agony perish,
For the swift arrow-heads all have in poison been dipped.

What they cannot carry or lead away they demolish,
And the hostile flames burn up the innocent cots.

Even when there is peace, the fear of war is impending;
None, with the ploughshare pressed, furrows the soil any more.

Either this region sees, or fears a foe that it sees not,
And the sluggish land slumbers in utter neglect.

No sweet grape lies hidden here in the shade of its vine-leaves,
No fermenting must fills and o'erflows the deep vats.

Apples the region denies; nor would Acontius have found here
Aught upon which to write words for his mistress to read.

Naked and barren plains without leaves or trees we behold here,—
Places, alas! unto which no happy man would repair.

Since then this mighty orb lies open so wide upon all sides,
Has this region been found only my prison to be?

TRISTIA, Book III, Elegy XII.

Now the zephyrs diminish the cold, and the year being ended,
Winter Maeotian seems longer than ever before;

And the Ram that bore unsafely the burden of Helle,
Now makes the hours of the day equal with those of the night.

Now the boys and the laughing girls the violet gather,
Which the fields bring forth, nobody sowing the seed.

Now the meadows are blooming with flowers of various colors,
And with untaught throats carol the garrulous birds.

Now the swallow, to shun the crime of her merciless mother,
Under the rafters builds cradles and dear little homes;

And the blade that lay hid, covered up in the furrows of Ceres,
Now from the tepid ground raises its delicate head.

Where there is ever a vine, the bud shoots forth from the tendrils,
But from the Getic shore distant afar is the vine!

Where there is ever a tree, on the tree the branches are swelling,
But from the Getic land distant afar is the tree!

Now it is holiday there in Rome, and to games in due order
Give place the windy wars of the vociferous bar.

Now they are riding the horses; with light arms now they are playing,
Now with the ball, and now round rolls the swift-flying hoop:

Now, when the young athlete with flowing oil is anointed,
He in the Virgin's Fount bathes, over-wearied, his limbs.

Thrives the stage; and applause, with voices at variance, thunders,
And the Theatres three for the three Forums resound.

Four times happy is he, and times without number is happy,
Who the city of Rome, uninterdicted, enjoys.

But all I see is the snow in the vernal sunshine dissolving,
And the waters no more delved from the indurate lake.

Nor is the sea now frozen, nor as before o'er the Ister
Comes the Sarmatian boor driving his stridulous cart.

Hitherward, nevertheless, some keels already are steering,
And on this Pontic shore alien vessels will be.

Eagerly shall I run to the sailor, and, having saluted,
Who he may be, I shall ask; wherefore and whence he hath come.

Strange indeed will it be, if he come not from regions adjacent,
And incautious unless ploughing the neighboring sea.

Rarely a mariner over the deep from Italy passes,
Rarely he comes to these shores, wholly of harbors devoid.

Whether he knoweth Greek, or whether in Latin he speaketh,
Surely on this account he the more welcome will be.

Also perchance from the mouth of the Strait and the waters Propontic,
Unto the steady South-wind, some one is spreading his sails.

Whosoever he is, the news he can faithfully tell me,
Which may become a part and an approach to the truth.

He, I pray, may be able to tell me the triumphs of Caesar,
Which he has heard of, and vows paid to the Latian Jove;

And that thy sorrowful head, Germania, thou, the rebellious,
Under the feet, at last, of the Great Captain hast laid.

Whoso shall tell me these things, that not to have seen will afflict me,
Forthwith unto my house welcomed as guest shall he be.

Woe is me! Is the house of Ovid in Scythian lands now?
And doth punishment now give me its place for a home?

Grant, ye gods, that Caesar make this not my house and my homestead,
But decree it to be only the inn of my pain.

FROM THE SPANISH

COPLAS DE MANRIQUE

O let the soul her slumbers break,
Let thought be quickened, and awake;
Awake to see
How soon this life is past and gone,
And death comes softly stealing on,
How silently!

Swiftly our pleasures glide away,

Our hearts recall the distant day
With many sighs;
The moments that are speeding fast
We heed not, but the past,—the past,
More highly prize.

Onward its course the present keeps,
Onward the constant current sweeps,
Till life is done;
And, did we judge of time aright,
The past and future in their flight
Would be as one.

Let no one fondly dream again,
That Hope and all her shadowy train
Will not decay;
Fleeting as were the dreams of old,
Remembered like a tale that's told,
They pass away.

Our lives are rivers, gliding free
To that unfathomed, boundless sea,
The silent grave!
Thither all earthly pomp and boast
Roll, to be swallowed up and lost
In one dark wave.

Thither the mighty torrents stray,
Thither the brook pursues its way,
And tinkling rill,
There all are equal; side by side
The poor man and the son of pride
Lie calm and still.

I will not here invoke the throng
Of orators and sons of song,
The deathless few;
Fiction entices and deceives,
And, sprinkled o'er her fragrant leaves,
Lies poisonous dew.

To One alone my thoughts arise,
The Eternal Truth, the Good and Wise,
To Him I cry,
Who shared on earth our common lot,
But the world comprehended not
His deity.

This world is but the rugged road
Which leads us to the bright abode
Of peace above;
So let us choose that narrow way,
Which leads no traveller's foot astray
From realms of love,

Our cradle is the starting-place,
Life is the running of the race,
We reach the goal
When, in the mansions of the blest,
Death leaves to its eternal rest
The weary soul.

Did we but use it as we ought,
This world would school each wandering thought
To its high state.
Faith wings the soul beyond the sky,
Up to that better world on high,
For which we wait.

Yes, the glad messenger of love,
To guide us to our home above,
The Saviour came;
Born amid mortal cares and fears.
He suffered in this vale of tears
A death of shame.

Behold of what delusive worth
The bubbles we pursue on earth,
The shapes we chase,
Amid a world of treachery!
They vanish ere death shuts the eye,
And leave no trace.

Time steals them from us, chances strange,
Disastrous accident, and change,
That come to all;
Even in the most exalted state,
Relentless sweeps the stroke of fate;
The strongest fall.

Tell me, the charms that lovers seek
In the clear eye and blushing cheek,
The hues that play
O'er rosy lip and brow of snow,
When hoary age approaches slow,
Ah; where are they?

The cunning skill, the curious arts,
The glorious strength that youth imparts
In life's first stage;
These shall become a heavy weight,
When Time swings wide his outward gate
To weary age.

The noble blood of Gothic name,
Heroes emblazoned high to fame,
In long array;
How, in the onward course of time,
The landmarks of that race sublime
Were swept away!

Some, the degraded slaves of lust,
Prostrate and trampled in the dust,
Shall rise no more;
Others, by guilt and crime, maintain
The scutcheon, that without a stain,
Their fathers bore.

Wealth and the high estate of pride,
With what untimely speed they glide,
How soon depart!
Bid not the shadowy phantoms stay,
The vassals of a mistress they,
Of fickle heart.

These gifts in Fortune's hands are found;
Her swift revolving wheel turns round,
And they are gone!
No rest the inconstant goddess knows,
But changing, and without repose,
Still hurries on.

Even could the hand of avarice save
Its gilded baubles till the grave
Reclaimed its prey,
Let none on such poor hopes rely;
Life, like an empty dream, flits by,
And where are they?

Earthly desires and sensual lust
Are passions springing from the dust,
They fade and die;
But in the life beyond the tomb,
They seal the immortal spirits doom

Eternally!

The pleasures and delights, which mask
In treacherous smiles life's serious task,
What are they, all,
But the fleet coursers of the chase,
And death an ambush in the race,
Wherein we fall?

No foe, no dangerous pass, we heed,
Brook no delay, but onward speed
With loosened rein;
And, when the fatal snare is near,
We strive to check our mad career,
But strive in vain.

Could we new charms to age impart,
And fashion with a cunning art
The human face,
As we can clothe the soul with light,
And make the glorious spirit bright
With heavenly grace,

How busily each passing hour
Should we exert that magic power,
What ardor show,
To deck the sensual slave of sin,
Yet leave the freeborn soul within,
In weeds of woe!

Monarchs, the powerful and the strong,
Famous in history and in song
Of olden time,
Saw, by the stern decrees of fate,
Their kingdoms lost, and desolate
Their race sublime.

Who is the champion? who the strong?
Pontiff and priest, and sceptred throng?
On these shall fall
As heavily the hand of Death,
As when it stays the shepherd's breath
Beside his stall.

I speak not of the Trojan name,
Neither its glory nor its shame
Has met our eyes;
Nor of Rome's great and glorious dead,

Though we have heard so oft, and read,
Their histories.

Little avails it now to know
Of ages passed so long ago,
Nor how they rolled;
Our theme shall be of yesterday,
Which to oblivion sweeps away,
Like day's of old.

Where is the King, Don Juan? Where
Each royal prince and noble heir
Of Aragon?
Where are the courtly gallantries?
The deeds of love and high emprise,
In battle done?

Tourney and joust, that charmed the eye,
And scarf, and gorgeous panoply,
And nodding plume,
What were they but a pageant scene?
What but the garlands, gay and green,
That deck the tomb?

Where are the high-born dames, and where
Their gay attire, and jewelled hair,
And odors sweet?
Where are the gentle knights, that came
To kneel, and breathe love's ardent flame,
Low at their feet?

Where is the song of Troubadour?
Where are the lute and gay tambour
They loved of yore?
Where is the mazy dance of old,
The flowing robes, inwrought with gold,
The dancers wore?

And he who next the sceptre swayed,
Henry, whose royal court displayed
Such power and pride;
O, in what winning smiles arrayed,
The world its various pleasures laid
His throne beside!

But O how false and full of guile
That world, which wore so soft a smile
But to betray!

She, that had been his friend before,
Now from the fated monarch tore
Her charms away.

The countless gifts, the stately walls,
The loyal palaces, and halls
All filled with gold;
Plate with armorial bearings wrought,
Chambers with ample treasures fraught
Of wealth untold;

The noble steeds, and harness bright,
And gallant lord, and stalwart knight,
In rich array,
Where shall we seek them now? Alas!
Like the bright dewdrops on the grass,
They passed away.

His brother, too, whose factious zeal
Usurped the sceptre of Castile,
Unskilled to reign;
What a gay, brilliant court had he,
When all the flower of chivalry
Was in his train!

But he was mortal; and the breath,
That flamed from the hot forge of Death,
Blasted his years;
Judgment of God! that flame by thee,
When raging fierce and fearfully,
Was quenched in tears!

Spain's haughty Constable, the true
And gallant Master, whom we knew
Most loved of all;
Breathe not a whisper of his pride,
He on the gloomy scaffold died,
Ignoble fall!

The countless treasures of his care,
His villages and villas fair,
His mighty power,
What were they all but grief and shame,
Tears and a broken heart, when came
The parting hour?

His other brothers, proud and high,
Masters, who, in prosperity,

Might rival kings;
Who made the bravest and the best
The bondsmen of their high behest,
Their underlings;

What was their prosperous estate,
When high exalted and elate
With power and pride?
What, but a transient gleam of light,
A flame, which, glaring at its height,
Grew dim and died?

So many a duke of royal name,
Marquis and count of spotless fame,
And baron brave,
That might the sword of empire wield,
All these, O Death, hast thou concealed
In the dark grave!

Their deeds of mercy and of arms,
In peaceful days, or war's alarms,
When thou dost show.
O Death, thy stern and angry face,
One stroke of thy all-powerful mace
Can overthrow.

Unnumbered hosts, that threaten nigh,
Pennon and standard flaunting high,
And flag displayed;
High battlements intrenched around,
Bastion, and moated wall, and mound,
And palisade,

And covered trench, secure and deep,
All these cannot one victim keep,
O Death, from thee,
When thou dost battle in thy wrath,
And thy strong shafts pursue their path
Unerringly.

O World! so few the years we live,
Would that the life which thou dost give
Were life indeed!
Alas! thy sorrows fall so fast,
Our happiest hour is when at last
The soul is freed.

Our days are covered o'er with grief,

And sorrows neither few nor brief
Veil all in gloom;
Left desolate of real good,
Within this cheerless solitude
No pleasures bloom.

Thy pilgrimage begins in tears,
And ends in bitter doubts and fears,
Or dark despair;
Midway so many toils appear,
That he who lingers longest here
Knows most of care.

Thy goods are bought with many a groan,
By the hot sweat of toil alone,
And weary hearts;
Fleet-footed is the approach of woe,
But with a lingering step and slow
Its form departs.

And he, the good man's shield and shade,
To whom all hearts their homage paid,
As Virtue's son,
Roderic Manrique, he whose name
Is written on the scroll of Fame,
Spain's champion;

His signal deeds and prowess high
Demand no pompous eulogy.
Ye saw his deeds!
Why should their praise in verse be sung?
The name, that dwells on every tongue,
No minstrel needs.

To friends a friend; how kind to all
The vassals of this ancient hall
And feudal fief!
To foes how stern a foe was he!
And to the valiant and the free
How brave a chief!

What prudence with the old and wise:
What grace in youthful gayeties;
In all how sage!
Benignant to the serf and slave,
He showed the base and falsely brave
A lion's rage.

His was Octavian's prosperous star,
The rush of Caesar's conquering car
At battle's call;
His, Scipio's virtue; his, the skill
And the indomitable will
Of Hannibal.

His was a Trajan's goodness, his
A Titus' noble charities
And righteous laws;
The arm of Hector, and the might
Of Tully, to maintain the right
In truth's just cause;

The clemency of Antonine,
Aurelius' countenance divine,
Firm, gentle, still;
The eloquence of Adrian,
And Theodosius' love to man,
And generous will;

In tented field and bloody fray,
An Alexander's vigorous sway
And stern command;
The faith of Constantine; ay, more,
The fervent love Camillus bore
His native land.

He left no well-filled treasury,
He heaped no pile of riches high,
Nor massive plate;
He fought the Moors, and, in their fall,
City and tower and castled wall
Were his estate.

Upon the hard-fought battle-ground,
Brave steeds and gallant riders found
A common grave;
And there the warrior's hand did gain
The rents, and the long vassal train,
That conquest gave.

And if, of old, his halls displayed
The honored and exalted grade
His worth had gained,
So, in the dark, disastrous hour,
Brothers and bondsmen of his power
His hand sustained.

After high deeds, not left untold,
In the stern warfare, which of old
'T was his to share,
Such noble leagues he made, that more
And fairer regions, than before,
His guerdon were.

These are the records, half effaced,
Which, with the hand of youth, he traced
On history's page;
But with fresh victories he drew
Each fading character anew
In his old age.

By his unrivalled skill, by great
And veteran service to the state,
By worth adored,
He stood, in his high dignity,
The proudest knight of chivalry,
Knight of the Sword.

He found his cities and domains
Beneath a tyrant's galling chains
And cruel power;
But by fierce battle and blockade,
Soon his own banner was displayed
From every tower.

By the tried valor of his hand,
His monarch and his native land
Were nobly served;
Let Portugal repeat the story,
And proud Castile, who shared the glory
His arms deserved.

And when so oft, for weal or woe,
His life upon the fatal throw
Had been cast down;
When he had served, with patriot zeal,
Beneath the banner of Castile,
His sovereign's crown;

And done such deeds of valor strong,
That neither history nor song
Can count them all;
Then, on Ocana's castled rock,
Death at his portal came to knock,

With sudden call,

Saying, "Good Cavalier, prepare
To leave this world of toil and care
With joyful mien;
Let thy strong heart of steel this day
Put on its armor for the fray,
The closing scene.

"Since thou hast been, in battle-strife,
So prodigal of health and life,
For earthly fame,
Let virtue nerve thy heart again;
Loud on the last stern battle-plain
They call thy name.

"Think not the struggle that draws near
Too terrible for man, nor fear
To meet the foe;
Nor let thy noble spirit grieve,
Its life of glorious fame to leave
On earth below.

"A life of honor and of worth
Has no eternity on earth,
'T is but a name;
And yet its glory far exceeds
That base and sensual life, which leads
To want and shame.

"The eternal life, beyond the sky,
Wealth cannot purchase, nor the high
And proud estate;
The soul in dalliance laid, the spirit
Corrupt with sin, shall not inherit
A joy so great.

"But the good monk, in cloistered cell,
Shall gain it by his book and bell,
His prayers and tears;
And the brave knight, whose arm endures
Fierce battle, and against the Moors
His standard rears.

"And thou, brave knight, whose hand has poured
The life-blood of the Pagan horde
O'er all the land,
In heaven shalt thou receive, at length,

The guerdon of thine earthly strength
And dauntless hand.

"Cheered onward by this promise sure,
Strong in the faith entire and pure
Thou dost profess,
Depart, thy hope is certainty,
The third, the better life on high
Shalt thou possess."

"O Death, no more, no more delay;
My spirit longs to flee away,
And be at rest;
The will of Heaven my will shall be,
I bow to the divine decree,
To God's behest.

"My soul is ready to depart,
No thought rebels, the obedient heart
Breathes forth no sigh;
The wish on earth to linger still
Were vain, when 't is God's sovereign will
That we shall die.

"O thou, that for our sins didst take
A human form, and humbly make
Thy home on earth;
Thou, that to thy divinity
A human nature didst ally
By mortal birth,

"And in that form didst suffer here
Torment, and agony, and fear,
So patiently;
By thy redeeming grace alone,
And not for merits of my own,
O, pardon me!"

As thus the dying warrior prayed,
Without one gathering mist or shade
Upon his mind;
Encircled by his family,
Watched by affection's gentle eye
So soft and kind;

His soul to Him, who gave it, rose;
God lead it to its long repose,
Its glorious rest!

And, though the warrior's sun has set,
Its light shall linger round us yet,
Bright, radiant, blest.

SONNETS

I

THE GOOD SHEPHERD

(EL BUEN PASTOR)

BY LOPE DE VEGA

Shepherd! who with thine amorous, sylvan song
Hast broken the slumber that encompassed me,
Who mad'st thy crook from the accursed tree,
On which thy powerful arms were stretched so long!
Lead me to mercy's ever-flowing fountains;
For thou my shepherd, guard, and guide shalt be;
I will obey thy voice, and wait to see
Thy feet all beautiful upon the mountains.
Hear, Shepherd! thou who for thy flock art dying,
O, wash away these scarlet sins, for thou
Rejoicest at the contrite sinner's vow.
O, wait! to thee my weary soul is crying,
Wait for me! Yet why ask it, when I see,
With feet nailed to the cross, thou 'rt waiting still for me!

II

TO-MORROW

(MANANA)

BY LOPE DE VEGA

Lord, what am I, that with unceasing care,
Thou didst seek after me, that thou didst wait
Wet with unhealthy dews, before my gate,
And pass the gloomy nights of winter there?
O strange delusion! that I did not greet
Thy blest approach, and O, to Heaven how lost,
If my ingratitude's unkindly frost

Has chilled the bleeding wounds upon thy feet.
How oft my guardian angel gently cried,
"Soul, from thy casement look, and thou shalt see
How he persists to knock and wait for thee!"
And, O! how often to that voice of sorrow,
"To-morrow we will open," I replied,
And when the morrow came I answered still "To-morrow."

III

THE NATIVE LAND

(EL PATRIO CIELO)

BY FRANCISCO DE ALDANA

Clear fount of light! my native land on high,
Bright with a glory that shall never fade!
Mansion of truth! without a veil or shade,
Thy holy quiet meets the spirit's eye.
There dwells the soul in its ethereal essence,
Gasping no longer for life's feeble breath;
But, sentinelled in heaven, its glorious presence
With pitying eye beholds, yet fears not, death.
Beloved country! banished from thy shore,
A stranger in this prison-house of clay,
The exiled spirit weeps and sighs for thee!
Heavenward the bright perfections I adore
Direct, and the sure promise cheers the way,
That, whither love aspires, there shall my dwelling be.

IV

THE IMAGE OF GOD

(LA IMAGEN DE DIOS)

BY FRANCISCO DE ALDANA

O Lord! who seest, from yon starry height,
Centred in one the future and the past,
Fashioned in thine own image, see how fast
The world obscures in me what once was bright!
Eternal Sun! the warmth which thou hast given,

To cheer life's flowery April, fast decays;
Yet in the hoary winter of my days,
Forever green shall be my trust in Heaven.
Celestial King! O let thy presence pass
Before my spirit, and an image fair
Shall meet that look of mercy from on high,
As the reflected image in a glass
Doth meet the look of him who seeks it there,
And owes its being to the gazer's eye.

V

THE BROOK

(A UN ARROYUELO)

ANONYMOUS

Laugh of the mountain!—lyre of bird and tree!
Pomp of the meadow! mirror of the morn!
The soul of April, unto whom are born
The rose and jessamine, leaps wild in thee!
Although, where'er thy devious current strays,
The lap of earth with gold and silver teems,
To me thy clear proceeding brighter seems
Than golden sands, that charm each shepherd's gaze.
How without guile thy bosom, all transparent
As the pure crystal, lets the curious eye
Thy secrets scan, thy smooth, round pebbles count!
How, without malice murmuring, glides thy current!
O sweet simplicity of days gone by!
Thou shun'st the haunts of man, to dwell in limpid fount!

ANCIENT SPANISH BALLADS

In the chapter with this title in Outre-Mer, besides Illustrations from Byron and Lockhart are the three following examples, contributed by Longfellow.

I

Rio Verde, Rio Verde!
Many a corpse is bathed in thee,
Both of Moors and eke of Christians,
Slain with swords most cruelly.

And thy pure and crystal waters
Dappled are with crimson gore;
For between the Moors and Christians
Long has been the fight and sore.

Dukes and Counts fell bleeding near thee,
Lords of high renown were slain,
Perished many a brave hidalgo
Of the noblemen of Spain.

II

"King Alfonso the Eighth, having exhausted his treasury in war, wishes to lay a tax of five farthings upon each of the Castillan hidalgos, in order to defray the expenses of a journey from Burgos to Cuenca. This proposition of the king was met with disdain by the noblemen who had been assembled on the occasion."

Don Nuno, Count of Lara,
In anger and in pride,
Forgot all reverence for the king,
And thus in wrath replied:

"Our noble ancestors," quoth he,
"Ne'er such a tribute paid;
Nor shall the king receive of us
What they have once gainsaid.

"The base-born soul who deems it just
May here with thee remain;
But follow me, ye cavaliers,
Ye noblemen of Spain."

Forth followed they the noble Count,
They marched to Glera's plain;
Out of three thousand gallant knights
Did only three remain.

They tied the tribute to their spears,
They raised it in the air,
And they sent to tell their lord the king
That his tax was ready there.

"He may send and take by force," said they,
"This paltry sum of gold;
But the goodly gift of liberty

Cannot be bought and sold."

III

"One of the finest of the historic ballads is that which describes Bernardo's march to Roncesvalles. He sallies forth 'with three thousand Leonese and more,' to protect the glory and freedom of his native land. From all sides, the peasantry of the land flock to the hero's standard."

The peasant leaves his plough afield,
The reaper leaves his hook,
And from his hand the shepherd-boy.
Lets fall the pastoral crook.

The young set up a shout of joy,
The old forget their years,
The feeble man grows stout of heart.
No more the craven fears.

All rush to Bernard's standard,
And on liberty they call;
They cannot brook to wear the yoke,
When threatened by the Gaul.

"Free were we born," 't is thus they cry
"And willingly pay we
The duty that we owe our king
By the divine decree.

"But God forbid that we obey
The laws of foreign knaves,
Tarnish the glory of our sires,
And make our children slaves.

"Our hearts have not so craven grown,
So bloodless all our veins,
So vigorless our brawny arms,
As to submit to chains.

"Has the audacious Frank, forsooth,
Subdued these seas and lands?
Shall he a bloodless victory have?
No, not while we have hands.

"He shall learn that the gallant Leonese
Can bravely fight and fall,
But that they know not how to yield;

They are Castilians all.

"Was it for this the Roman power
Of old was made to yield
Unto Numantia's valiant hosts
On many a bloody field?

"Shall the bold lions that have bathed
Their paws in Libyan gore,
Crouch basely to a feebler foe,
And dare the strife no more?

"Let the false king sell town and tower,
But not his vassals free;
For to subdue the free-born soul
No royal power hath he!"

Henry Wadsworth Longfellow – A Short Biography

Henry Wadsworth Longfellow was born on February 27th, 1807 in Portland, Maine (then part of Massachusetts) to Stephen Longfellow and Zilpah (nee Wadsworth) Longfellow. His father was a lawyer, and his maternal grandfather, Peleg Wadsworth, was a general in the American Revolutionary War and a Member of Congress.

It was a large family. Longfellow was the second of eight children; his siblings were Stephen (1805), Elizabeth (1808), Anne (1810), Alexander (1814), Mary (1816), Ellen (1818) and Samuel (1819).

Longfellow attended a dame school at the age of three and by age six was enrolled at the private Portland Academy. He was very studious and quickly became fluent in Latin. His mother encouraged his love of reading and learning and introduced him to many literary classics.

He published his first poem, a patriotic four-stanza affair entitled "The Battle of Lovell's Pond", in the Portland Gazette on November 17, 1820. He remained at the Portland Academy until he was fourteen. As a child, he spent much of his summers at his grandfather Peleg's farm in the nearby town of Hiram.

In the fall of 1822, the 15-year-old Longfellow enrolled at Bowdoin College in Brunswick, Maine. His grandfather was a founder of the college and his father a trustee. Here he met and befriended Nathaniel Hawthorne. Longfellow was already thinking of a career in literature. In his senior year he wrote to his father: "I will not disguise it in the least... the fact is, I most eagerly aspire after future eminence in literature, my whole soul burns most ardently after it, and every earthly thought centers in it... I am almost confident in believing, that if I can ever rise in the world it must be by the exercise of my talents in the wide field of literature."

Poetry was the writing form he felt most at ease with and he offered poems to many newspapers and magazines. Between January 1824 and graduation in 1825, he had almost 40 poems published, over half of which were in the short-lived Boston periodical The United States Literary Gazette.

When Longfellow graduated, he was ranked a pleasing fourth in the class, and had been elected to Phi Beta Kappa. He was quickly offered the post of professor of modern languages at his alma mater.

Accounts suggest that part of the requirement of acceptance was to tour Europe to become more immersed in both languages and cultures. Longfellow began his tour of Europe in May 1826 aboard the ship Cadmus. His travels in Europe would last three years and cost his father the princely sum of $2,604.24. He visited France, Spain, Italy, Germany and England before returning to the United States in mid-August 1829.

His stock of languages now included French, Spanish, Portuguese, and German, and impressively, mostly without any formal instruction.

On August 27th, 1829, he wrote to the president of Bowdoin that he was turning down the professorship because he considered the $600 salary "disproportionate to the duties required". The trustees countered by raising the salary to $800 and an additional $100 to serve as the college's librarian, a post which required only one hour's attention a day.

On September 14th, 1831, Longfellow married Mary Storer Potter, a childhood friend from Portland. The couple settled in Brunswick. Longfellow now published several non-fiction and fiction prose pieces inspired by his friend Washington Irving, whom he had met in Madrid during his travels, these included "The Indian Summer" and "The Bald Eagle" in 1833.

During his years teaching at the college, he translated textbooks in French, Italian and Spanish; his first published book was in 1833, a translation of the poetry of the medieval Spanish poet Jorge Manrique. A travel book, Outre-Mer: A Pilgrimage Beyond the Sea, was first published in serial form before a book edition in 1835.

In December 1834, Longfellow received a letter from Josiah Quincy III, president of Harvard College, offering him the Smith Professorship of Modern Languages with the condition that he first spend a year or so abroad. The Longfellow's set off for Europe. He would now be able to add German, Dutch, Danish, Swedish, Finnish, and Icelandic to his repertoire of languages.

During the trip they discovered that Mary was pregnant. Sadly, in October 1835, she miscarried some six months into the pregnancy. Then followed several weeks of illness and at the age of 22 on November 29th, 1835 she died. Longfellow had her body embalmed, placed in a lead coffin itself inside an oak coffin which was then shipped to Mount Auburn Cemetery near Boston. He wrote movingly "One thought occupies me night and day... She is dead—She is dead! All day I am weary and sad".

Back in the United States, Longfellow took up the professorship at Harvard. He was required to live in Cambridge, close to the campus and rented rooms at the Craigie House in the spring of 1837. The home, built in 1759, had once been the headquarters of George Washington during the Siege of Boston.

Longfellow now felt able to publish again, starting with the collection Voices of the Night in 1839. It was mainly comprised of translations together with nine original poems and seven poems written back in his teenage years.

His romantic interests also began to surface again. He had begun to court Frances 'Fanny' Appleton, daughter of the Boston industrialist Nathan Appleton. At first, the independent-minded Appleton was not interested in marriage but Longfellow was determined. In July 1839, he wrote to a friend: "Victory hangs doubtful. The lady says she will not! I say she shall! It is not pride, but the madness of passion".

In late 1839, Longfellow published Hyperion, a book in prose inspired by his trips abroad and his still unsuccessful courtship of Fanny Appleton. Amidst this, Longfellow fell into "periods of neurotic depression with moments of panic" and required a six-month leave of absence from Harvard to attend a health spa in the former Marienberg Benedictine Convent at Boppard in Germany.

Ballads and Other Poems was published in 1841 and included "The Village Blacksmith" and "The Wreck of the Hesperus". His reputation as a poet, and a commercial one at that, was set.

Longfellow published a play in 1842, The Spanish Student, based on his memories from his time in Spain in the 1820s. A small collection, Poems on Slavery, was also published in 1842. This was Longfellow's first public support of abolitionism. However, as Longfellow himself said, the poems were "so mild that even a Slaveholder might read them without losing his appetite for breakfast". The New England Anti-Slavery Association, however, was satisfied enough with the intent of the collection to reprint it for their own distribution.

On May 10th, 1843, after seven years in pursuit, Longfellow received a letter from Fanny Appleton agreeing to marry him. He was elated and immediately walked 90 minutes to meet her at her house.

Nathan Appleton bought the Craigie House as a wedding present to the pair. Longfellow lived there for the rest of his life. His love for Fanny is evident from Longfellow's only love poem, the sonnet "The Evening Star", written in October 1845:

"O my beloved, my sweet Hesperus!
My morning and my evening star of love!"

He once attended a ball without her and said, "The lights seemed dimmer, the music sadder, the flowers fewer, and the women less fair."

Longfellow and Fanny had six children: Charles Appleton (1844), Ernest Wadsworth (1845), Fanny (1847, who died in infancy), Alice Mary (1850), Edith (1853), and Anne Allegra (1855).

Aware of his growing stature and his ability to influence others he also encouraged and supported many other translators. In 1845, he published The Poets and Poetry of Europe, a large 800-page compendium of translated works by other writers. Longfellow intended the anthology "to bring together, into a compact and convenient form, as large an amount as possible of those English translations which are scattered through many volumes, and are not accessible to the general reader".

On November 1st, 1847, the epic poem Evangeline was published.

Longfellow's literary income was now becoming quite substantial: in 1840, he had made $219 but by 1850 it had grown to a very promising $1,900.

On June 14th, 1853, Longfellow held a farewell dinner party at his Cambridge home for his great friend Nathaniel Hawthorne, who was preparing to move overseas.

In 1854, Longfellow retired from Harvard, devoting himself entirely to writing. He would be awarded an honorary doctorate of laws from Harvard in 1859.

The Song of Haiwatha, his epic poem, and perhaps his best known and enjoyed work was published in 1855.

On a hot July 9th day, 1861, Fanny was putting several locks of her children's hair into an envelope and making attempts to seal it with hot sealing wax while Longfellow took a nap. The circumstances of what happened next vary but the actuality is that Fanny's dress caught fire. Her screams awakened Longfellow who rushed to help her and threw a rug over her and stifled the flames with his own body as best he could, but Fanny was already horrifically burned.

A doctor was called and Fanny was taken to her room to recover. She was in and out of consciousness throughout the night and was also administered ether. The next morning, July 10th, 1861, she died shortly after 10 o'clock after asking for a cup of coffee.

Longfellow, in his effort to save her had also been badly burned and was unable to attend her funeral. His facial injuries required he stopped shaving. The ensuing beard now became the quintessential look that everyone remembers from pictures.

Devastated, he never fully recovered and sometimes resorted to laudanum and ether to ease the pain. He worried he would go insane and begged "not to be sent to an asylum" and noted that he was "inwardly bleeding to death". In the sonnet "The Cross of Snow" (1879), which he wrote eighteen years later he wrote:

"Such is the cross I wear upon my breast
These eighteen years, through all the changing scenes
And seasons, changeless since the day she died".

Longfellow spent several years translating Dante Alighieri's epic poem, The Divine Comedy. To aid him in perfecting the translation and reviewing proofs, he invited several friends to weekly meetings every Wednesday from 1864. This became known as the "Dante Club", and regulars included William Dean Howells, James Russell Lowell, Charles Eliot Norton and other occasional guests. The full three-volume translation was published in the spring of 1867, though Longfellow would continue to revise it. It was wildly popular and was re-printed four times in its first year.

By 1868, Longfellow's annual income was over a staggering $48,000.

Longfellow was also part of a group of Poets who became known as The Fireside Poets. The group included Longfellow, William Cullen Bryant, John Greenleaf Whittier, James Russell Lowell, and Oliver Wendell Holmes Snr. Occasionally Ralph Waldo Emerson is also placed among their number. The name "Fireside Poets" derives from poetry reading as a collective family entertainment of the times.

During the 1860s, Longfellow, still a committed abolitionist, also hoped for a coming together, a reconciliation, between the north and south after the dark days of the Civil War. When his son was wounded during the war, he wrote the poem "Christmas Bells", later the basis of the carol I Heard the Bells on Christmas Day.

In 1874, Samuel Cutler Ward helped him sell the poem "The Hanging of the Crane" to the New York Ledger for $3,000; it was the highest price ever paid for a poem. An astonishing sum. But Longfellow was worth it. His fame and audience were widespread and devoted.

Continuing in his hopes for a better and more united America he wrote in his journal in 1878: "I have only one desire; and that is for harmony, and a frank and honest understanding between North and South". Longfellow, despite his aversion to public speaking, took up an offer from Joshua Chamberlain to speak at his fiftieth reunion at Bowdoin College. Here he read the poem "Morituri Salutamus" so quietly that few could hear.

On August 22th, 1879, a female admirer who seemed to know little about his history, traveled to Longfellow's house in Cambridge and, unaware to whom she was speaking, asked Longfellow: "Is this the house where Longfellow was born?" Longfellow told her it was not. The visitor then asked if he had died here. "Not yet", he replied.

Much of Longfellow's work is recognized for its melody-like musicality. As he says, "what a writer asks of his reader is not so much to like as to listen".

Longfellow, like many others of the period, called for the development of high quality American literature. In his work, Kavanagh, a character says: "We want a national literature commensurate with our mountains and rivers... We want a national epic that shall correspond to the size of the country... We want a national drama in which scope shall be given to our gigantic ideas and to the unparalleled activity of our people... In a word, we want a national literature altogether shaggy and unshorn, that shall shake the earth, like a herd of buffaloes thundering over the prairies."

As a translator Longfellow was very impressive. His translation of Dante's The Divine Comedy became a requirement for those who wanted to be a part of high culture.

In 1874, Longfellow oversaw a 31-volume anthology called Poems of Places, collecting poems of several geographical locations; Europe, Asia, and the Arabian countries. It was a work of great educational endeavor but Emerson was disappointed and is said to have told Longfellow: "The world is expecting better things of you than this... You are wasting time that should be bestowed upon original production".

At this point in his life Longfellow could look back and see that his early collections, Voices of the Night and Ballads and Other Poems, had made him instantly popular. The New-Yorker called him "one of the very few in our time who has successfully aimed in putting poetry to its best and sweetest uses". The Southern Literary Messenger immediately put Longfellow "among the first of our American poets".

The rapidity with which American readers embraced Longfellow was unparalleled in publishing history in the United States. His popularity spread throughout Europe, his poems translated into Italian, French, German, and other languages.

Longfellow was the most popular poet of his day. As a friend once wrote to him, "no other poet was so fully recognized in his lifetime". Some of his works including "Paul Revere's Ride" and "The Song of

Haiwatha" may have rewritten the facts but became essential parts of the American psyche and culture. He was so admired that on his 70th birthday in 1877 the atmosphere was that of a national holiday, with parades, speeches, and, of course, the reading of his poems.

Over the years, Longfellow's reputation came to include his personality; he was a gentle, placid, poetic soul. James Russell Lowell said, Longfellow had an "absolute sweetness, simplicity, and modesty". The reality was that Longfellow's life was much more difficult than was assumed. He suffered from neuralgia, which caused him constant pain, and poor eyesight. The difficulties of coping with the loss of two wives also took its toll. He was very quiet, reserved, and private; in later years, he became increasingly unsocial and avoided leaving home if he could.

In March 1882, Longfellow went to bed with severe stomach pain. He endured the pain for several days with the help of opium.

Henry Wadsworth Longfellow died, surrounded by family, on Friday, March 24th, 1882. He had been suffering from peritonitis.

He is buried with both of his wives at Mount Auburn Cemetery in Cambridge, Massachusetts. At Longfellow's funeral, his friend Ralph Waldo Emerson called him "a sweet and beautiful soul".

At the time of his death, his estate was valued at $356,320.

In 1884, Longfellow became the first non-British writer for whom a sculpted bust was placed in Poet's Corner of Westminster Abbey in London; he remains the sole American poet thus represented.

Henry Wadsworth Longfellow – A Concise Bibliography

Outre-Mer: A Pilgrimage Beyond the Sea (Travelogue) (1835)
Hyperion, a Romance (1839)
The Spanish Student. A Play in Three Acts (1843)
Evangeline: A Tale of Acadie (poem) (1847)
Kavanagh (1849)
The Golden Legend (poem) (1851)
The Song of Hiawatha (poem) (1855)
The New England Tragedies (1868)
The Divine Tragedy (1871)
Christus: A Mystery (1872)
Aftermath (poem) (1873)
The Arrow and the Song (poem)

Poetry Collections

Voices of the Night (1839)
Ballads & Other Poems (1841)
Poems on Slavery (1842)

The Belfry of Bruges & Other Poems (1845)
The Seaside and the Fireside (1850)
The Poetical Works of Henry Wadsworth Longfellow (1852)
The Courtship of Miles Standish & Other Poems (1858)
Tales of a Wayside Inn (1863)
Birds of Passage (1863)
Household Poems (1865)
Flower-de-Luce (1867)
Three Books of Song (1872)
The Masque of Pandora & Other Poems (1875)
Kéramos & Other Poems (1878)
Ultima Thule (1880)
In the Harbor (1882)
Michel Angelo: A Fragment (incomplete; published posthumously)

Translations

Coplas de Don Jorge Manrique (Translation from Spanish) (1833)
Dante's Divine Comedy (Translation) (1867)

Anthologies

Poets and Poetry of Europe (Translations) (1845)
The Waif (1845)
Poems of Places (1874)

Printed in Great Britain
by Amazon